RV
REAL ESTATE
INCOME

Discover How You Can Live The RV Lifestyle Of Your Dreams With Virtual Real Estate Related Activities

Ben Souchek

This book is Copyright © 2016 Ben Souchek ("Souchek"). All Rights Reserved. Published in the United States of America. The legal notices, disclosures, and disclaimers within this book are copyrighted by the Law Office of Michael E. Young PLLC and licensed for use by Souchek in this book. All rights reserved.

No part of this book may be reproduced or transmitted in any form or by any means, electronic or mechanical, including photocopying, recording, or by an information storage and retrieval system -- except by a reviewer who may quote brief passages in a review to be printed in a magazine, newspaper, blog, or website -- without permission in writing from Souchek. For information, please contact Souchek by e-mail using the contact form found at RVRealEstateIncome.com, or by mail at P.O. Box 22339, Lincoln, Nebraska 68542 USA.

For more information, please read the "Disclosures and Disclaimers" section at the end of this book.

First Edition, November 2016

Published by The Sierra Group LLC, a Nebraska limited liability company ("Sierra Group").

ISBN: 1540300668
ISBN 13: 9781540300669

RV REAL ESTATE INCOME

1	Introduction	1
2	Goals and Plans	5
3	Selecting A Market Area	7

• Section 1   Active Activity Income   13

4	Buying & Selling Houses	15
5	Wholesaling Houses	19
6	Generate Leads for Real Estate Agents & Investors	23
7	Provide Virtual Services for Real Estate Agents & Investors	29
8	Create Content for Real Estate Agents & Investors	33

• Section 2   Passive Income Generation   35

9	Buying Rental Houses	37
10	Owning Parts of Rental Houses	41
11	Private Lending	43
12	Buying Tax Liens	47
13	Get a Real Estate License to Generate Referral Income	51

• Section 3   Bonus Resources   55

14	Financing Options When Buying Houses	57
15	Locating Properties to Buy and Resell or Hold as Rentals	63
16	Tax Benefits	67
17	Summary	69

About the Author	71
Disclosures and Disclaimers	72
Notes	80

1

INTRODUCTION

Are you one of the many RV enthusiasts in the country? Would you like to spend more time RVing, RV full time, have a nicer RV, enjoy the time you spend RVing now more, or just be able to get your first RV and start living a more enjoyable lifestyle?

What's stopping you? If you're like many people, the answer is the need of more income.

Before writing this, I started searching online for what others are doing to create or supplement their income. Unfortunately what I found was mostly ways to live a "cheap" RV lifestyle or ways to work conventional jobs while living in an RV. I also read plenty of information about virtual jobs and job sites where a person only needs a computer and internet connection, but most of the information was theoretical and not actual ways that people were generating an income. This is not what I was looking for when wanting to find new ways to create an enjoyable RV lifestyle.

For the last couple of years (as of this writing in July of 2016) my wife and I have been thinking of purchasing an RV due to family issues that do not allow us to travel "conventionally" at this time.

I will confess to you, I knew that if I were going to spend time in an RV, I wanted to live well.

So last winter we ordered, and this spring took delivery of, a new 2016 Newmar Mountain Aire. We were able to minimally customize the drawer "wall" in the bedroom area to have a desk so that I could work in the RV while my wife and 8 year old son are at the front of the coach.

Our goal is to be able to spend as much time as we'd like to travel and choose when to travel, although I don't see us as full timers, at least not for a long time.

The reason I am writing this is to share what I have done for almost 20 years as an occupation, which is now allowing us to live our RV lifestyle.

For almost 20 years I have bought and sold or bought and kept single family houses as rentals. I also have a real estate license but do not "act" as a real estate salesperson or broker.

At this time, my company buys houses in 3 different cities (other than the city we live in). And with some great assistants, doesn't require a lot of my time, and the time it does require can be done wherever I am (including in our RV).

No, I am not here to teach or sell you a course on how to buy and sell real estate. Although if you have an interest in that, I will provide some information about doing just that as well as providing resources to assist with real estate acquisition and investment. I will have some of these resources at www.RVRealEstateIncome.com.

What I want to share with you is how various aspects and involvement in real estate that I have learned in 20 years can help fund your desired RV lifestyle.

There are essentially two aspects of real estate activities that I will discuss. Active and passive activities. The active activities are ones that do require your time, effort, computer, phone, and internet connection that can be done from the comfort of your RV. The passive items are investments, that once made, will create a passive income for you.

Why should you have an interest in this book about generating income with real estate? I truly believe it can be the difference between living the lifestyle you now live and having the RV lifestyle that you want and dream of.

With that, lets get started!

2

GOALS AND PLANS

If you haven't already, the first thing you need to do is to create a yearly and monthly budget of your spending, your current income, what you'd like to be spending, and what your desired income needs to be to create the RV lifestyle you desire.

Depending on your goals, you may need no additional income, a little additional income, or an amount that doesn't seem realistic to achieve.

No matter where you are financially, you need to know where you are, and then create goals and a plan to get to where you want to be.

Having well defined goals is critical to getting to where you want to be financially.

Knowing how to invest funds that you may have in retirement plans or other savings vehicles is also critical. Knowing how to invest and generate a 6% to 12% return on your money instead of having those same funds sitting in a bank account earning ¼ of a percent can make a huge difference in what kind of an RV lifestyle you can live.

To make the math easy, $1,000,000 earning 1% a year will only generate $10,000 a year, or less than $1,000 per month. However that same $1,000,000 invested at 6% per year will generate $60,000 per year, or $5,000 per month. And although it may seem impossible in the current financial climate to earn 12% on your money, it is possible, and you can do the math to see what that would accomplish for you.

Knowing how to invest your funds can mean the difference between living a "cheap" RV lifestyle and living the RV lifestyle of your dreams.

If you are not at a place that your savings and investments can provide the RV lifestyle you want, knowing how much income you need to generate each month with the Active activities or implementing the Passive activity ideas will give you an idea as you read the following chapters.

Getting the knowledge needed to execute your plan and accomplish your goals is also an important piece of the puzzle. My goal is that this book will provide a good starting point for that.

3

SELECTING A MARKET AREA

In addition to the goals and plans mentioned last chapter, you need to also research and select a market or markets that you will want to focus on, especially if you are buying and selling or buying and holding houses as rentals.

In this chapter we will cover some of the criteria for selecting a market area to do business in. If you don't plan to buy and resell or buy and hold houses, the market area may not be as important, but you will still want to know what market areas other investors or speculators will want or should be in.

Initially it may make sense to look at areas that you would like to spend time or more time at. But know that you can do a number of activities mentioned in this book from anywhere your RV is, assuming you have good phone and internet access.

Although it may be convenient to initially look at what you would consider your "home" market, you need to look at several additional items to determine the best markets to target.

Growth and stability of the city and or state, multiple exit strategies available, price affordability, similarity to current market area, adequate amount of housing stock to fit your plans and goals, ability to implement marketing to reach your desired potential home sellers, does the state have state income taxes that you will need to pay, other taxes associated with doing business, do you need to register your company in the state, other laws and regulations.

Growth and stability of the city and/or state should be a consideration. Is the market area growing in population or losing population? There are currently areas in the country that are losing population due to various reasons. There are also parts of the country where population is growing.

There will always be shifts in population, but knowing which areas are growing is necessary especially when looking at a long term investment perspective. I would much rather own rental property in areas where the demand for housing is increasing instead of decreasing. You may be able to buy houses at more "affordable" prices in population decreasing areas, but there is most likely a reason for that.

There are areas in the south and southeast parts of the country such as Texas and Florida that are growing and have good business climates (and good climates in general) that are attracting more people. There are other parts of the country that seem to be repelling people. And there are parts of the country such as where I do business, in Omaha, Nebraska and the Kansas City areas that have slow growth and are very stable.

I also want to consider the ability to have multiple exit strategies (buy and resell, wholesale, or buy and hold for rental) when considering an area to do business in. The areas and price range that I purchase houses in is typically what would be considered a first time homebuyer house. The price range of these houses would generally be less than the median price of houses in a given area. There would typically be more availability and demand for these types of houses.

This price range of house allows for a much better return on investment, when keeping houses for rentals, than houses at or above the median price range of houses in an area.

A person can possibly make an even better return on houses priced well below this first homebuyer house range, but there are typically challenges with this type of rental in the form of lower quality tenants and more maintenance for the rentals. The ability to resell a house and less price appreciation is also usually associated with these houses.

There are some great, more expensive (and much less expensive) communities in most metro areas, but I prefer the areas that I am more comfortable doing business in and having the exit strategies that the above price range affords me.

Just about all of the houses I target and work with are in the first time home buyer range, typically $100,000 to $150,000 retail price range. In my areas the median price of houses are approximately $175,000.

I have purchased houses in a price range slightly higher than this first time home buyer range and either sold or kept as rentals. This will hopefully attract a better quality tenant and be a better quality long term investment, but the cash return on the value of the property will likely not be quite as high as the lower priced houses. Part of my longer term goals is to have more higher quality rental houses than I currently have.

Adequate amount of housing stock to fit your plans and goals. There are some communities that have been developed in just the last 5 or 10 years. It would be difficult to find "run down" or distressed houses in these areas.

At the other end of the spectrum there are neighborhoods that were developed 70 or more years ago. Houses in these areas are more likely to have issues that I would prefer to avoid such as foundation problems, needing new plumbing, electrical, or other functional obsolescence items.

My preference is to target neighborhoods with houses that are 20 to 35 years old. These neighborhoods have the possibility that some people have not improved the house since it was built. Houses are also new enough to be built after 1978, so lead based paint won't be an issue. These are especially houses that I would prefer to keep as rentals compared to older houses.

These and older houses may still be good for wholesaling or flipping, but I would prefer not to hold the older houses for rentals.

Having a plan and goals of what you want to accomplish in a market is necessary so that you will know what states, cities, and neighborhoods to target.

Ability to implement marketing to reach your target market. There are some communities that have marketing mediums such as newspapers, local publications, TV and radio stations, etc. that are just more affordable to reach my target home owner market.

I have encountered metro wide newspapers in cities with a population of approximately 250,000 that cost as much as in cities with 750,000.

Researching a potential market to determine how you can reach potential home sellers and how much it will cost is a necessary part of knowing if you have a good market to target.

Tax issues. Does the state that you are considering doing business in have state income taxes? If all other issues are equal, I would much rather do business in a state with no income tax.

Are the taxes for buying and selling houses expensive compared to other areas? There are some states that are much less expensive than others to buy and sell real estate. Recording fees, doc stamps, etc. can effect your business, especially looking at the costs over time.

Do you need to register your company in the state you are considering doing business in? Some states will require that you register your business, so be aware of the regulations in those states.

Other laws and regulations. Some states are more strict than others about items such as paying "bird dogs" to locate houses or refer deals to you.

Ensure that you know the laws and regulations of the markets you are doing business in so that you don't have unexpected, unpleasant surprises.

If you have located a few geographic or metro areas that look like good targets, I would then recommend contacting several real estate agents and property management companies in those areas.

Although real estate agents are prohibited by law from telling you what areas may be "bad" they can provide information on which neighborhoods or subdivisions may be more salable or in demand for certain price ranges. They can also direct you to resources that can provide a better pictures of specific neighborhoods or subdivisions.

Property management companies can likewise tell you which neighborhoods and subdivisions are in more demand for rentals. They can tell you the types of houses with what amenities are in demand, such as a 3 or 4 bedroom, size of yard, garage, etc. They should also be able to tell you the approximate rent ranges for various types/sizes of houses and neighborhoods.

After speaking with the real estate agents and property management companies, always perform your own research to confirm what you have been told.

Section 1

ACTIVE ACTIVITY INCOME

In this first section we will discuss the different ways to generate income that require an "active" involvement from you. And although they require your active participation, for the most part they can be done from the comfort of your RV.

I would highly recommend that you spend time looking at houses when you are getting started especially if you are planning on purchasing, but you can do most of the activities from your RV.

Knowing values of houses in their current "as is" condition, updated or "nice" condition, and costs of repairs and updates to make them "nice" are critical to your success.

4

BUYING & SELLING HOUSES

One of the most common ways to participate in real estate, and the primary way that I have for more than 20 years, is to buy and resell (flip) houses.

Why discuss flipping houses in a book discussing ways to earn income from your RV? Because you can, of course. In my book Virtual Real Estate Wealth I discuss how I started my career of buying and selling houses while living on my family farm and then later (and currently) living in Lincoln, Nebraska and "flipping" houses in the Omaha, Kansas City, and Tampa metro areas.

This may not be something you jump to right away or even need or want to do depending on your goals, but it is something you can do if you choose to.

If you are doing any of the other real estate items mentioned in this book you are likely to run across situations where this chapter will be applicable.

The thought of buying & selling houses may be daunting, but there are other chapters in this book and resources that will provide the pieces to this puzzle. Also know that the scope of this book will not provide the necessary room or information needed to know all you need to flip houses, but it is a start.

One of the biggest reasons to want to have some knowledge of flipping houses is that each "deal" can be worth $10,000 to $20,000 or more. What would doing just 1 of these transactions a month do for your desired RV lifestyle?

Whether you buy and sell, wholesale, or buy and hold houses, you will generally start with the same basic information and tasks discussed in other chapters of this book.

A key to being able to buy houses in general is having the ability to have access to cash and close quickly, or when the seller wants.

One primary reason that a seller will sell a house for a perceived "discount" is that they don't want to wait the usual time it takes to put a house on the market, find a buyer, and wait for the buyer to secure a loan.

Some other reasons that a home owner may want to sell in a non traditional way (not using a real estate agent) are; House needs too many repairs that the owner doesn't want to do or have the money for, a life event such as a death in the family or divorce, doesn't want strangers coming into their house, doesn't want the hassle of having agents call at inconvenient times to show the house, the "catch 22" of not wanting to sell until they can move to a new home or moving to a new home before having their house sold, or just wanting to be in more control of the entire transaction of selling their house.

Again, there is more information pertinent to buying and selling houses in other chapters of this book, as well as at www.RVRealEstateIncome.com

Just know that with education and taking action, you can buy and sell houses from your RV.

5

WHOLESALING HOUSES

Wholesaling houses requires most of the tasks and abilities as buying and selling houses but does not require you to actually buy the house.

Wholesaling requires finding a "deal," getting a contract to buy the property, and then selling that contract to an end buyer that will actually close and purchase the property.

Most new investors and real estate entrepreneurs get their start in real estate with wholesaling.

This allows a person to gain knowledge on the various aspects of working with real estate such as finding deals, marketing to find deals, determining current and potential values of houses, determining costs needed to rehab and repair houses, and finding buyers without the financial risks of having to actually purchase houses.

The profit on these types of transactions are typically $2,000 to $5,000 per house. If the after repaired value of the house is above $100,000 or the deal is extremely good, the wholesaler may make a bigger profit. When wholesaling a house, enough profit has to be left in the transaction as an incentive for a buyer to purchase the contract and take on the financial risk of buying the house.

Besides finding and securing the deal, the other primary aspect of wholesaling is to have ready and able buyers that can make a decision to buy and have the ability to close quickly when you bring them a deal.

There are a few different ways that you can find buyers for your wholesale deals.

One way would be to call other investors in an area that you are targeting. Investors in an area will put up "bandit" signs, advertise on billboards, have web sites that you can search for online, yellow page ads, or be listed with local real estate investment clubs.

Another way would be to search public records such as the county assessor or treasurer records in a targeted county to check for non owner occupied owners of multiple houses. When you find owners of multiple houses that have a different mailing address than the property address, it would indicate a good potential buyer of other houses that you could locate in those areas.

Real estate agents and property managers may also be a good source of potential buyers. The agents may want a commission if they refer a buyer to you, but it may be well worth it if they can provide you with an actual good quality buyer for your wholesale deals.

I would recommend you be able to provide the approximate ARV (After Repaired Value or "Retail" value) with comparables to support this value, and the approximate costs of repairs or rehab it will take to attain the ARV.

The more information you can provide about the property, pictures, etc. the easier decision a potential buyer will have to determine if they have an interest in purchasing the property

You will want to ensure that you can offer the property at a price that includes a profit for yourself and is attractive to a potential buyer.

Know that most buyers will want to Net approximately 15% to 20%, or a minimum of $20,000, of their selling price when they are considering buying a property. To put it another way, if a house will sell for $100,000 in Retail condition, they will want to Net approximately $20,000 after all expenses, including the purchase, updates or rehab, holding costs, selling expenses, etc.

ARV (After Repaired Value) :	$ 100,000
Subtract Repairs :	20,000
Buyer Profit :	20,000
Holding & Sales Costs :	15,000
Total Costs :	($ 55,000)
Wholesale Profit :	($ 5,000)
Maximum offer to Seller :	$ 40,000)

This will give you an idea of what the numbers have to look like to be a "deal."

Another way to determine this amount is to call and ask actual investor/buyers of houses what they need the numbers to be in order for them to be interested in buying a house. Or what a "deal" needs to look like for them to be interested in buying.

Although your initial thoughts may be that the price you would get a contract to purchase the house is very low, know that this is what the number has to be if it's going to be a "deal." Also realize that not every seller will work with these numbers, but there are sellers that will.

For additional information on wholesaling houses, check out RVRealEstateIncome.com

6

GENERATE LEADS FOR REAL ESTATE AGENTS & INVESTORS

One Active task that you can do to generate income without the risks and knowledge needed to buy or wholesale houses is to generate leads for real estate agents and investors.

After 20 years of buying and selling houses, the one thing I know is that it is critical to the success of a real estate business to be able to generate leads of home owners that want to sell.

Agents and Investors are always trying to generate leads of home sellers. How can you profit from this need?

There are a few different ways that we will discuss in this chapter. Direct mail campaigns, telephone or telemarketing campaigns, online marketing campaigns.

Although it may seem unrealistic to implement a direct mail campaign from your RV, it is possible with today's technology.

With a direct mail campaign, you need to first identify home owners that may be likely to want or need to sell their house. A few examples of these would be a death in the family (probate would be included in this), divorce, needing to downsize (maybe to buy an RV and travel!), house is in disrepair and may have code enforcement violations filed against it, Expired listings from the MLS (Multiple Listing Service), etc. For a larger list of reasons why home owners may want to sell their house, check out RVRealEstateIncome.com

Some of these lists you are able to purchase from list brokers, obtain from county government offices, or build yourself by looking up information online. The one thing I can tell you is that the more difficult the list is to obtain, the better the list is. If the information is difficult to obtain to compile a list, most people are too lazy to do what it takes to create that particular list.

When you have created a list, I use Microsoft Excel, the list can then be uploaded into an online mailing service such as Click2Mail.com that will mail out any size list (literally a few post cards to thousands of post cards) in the form that you want. You can then create a post card, letter, or other print media that they will mail for you. With Click2Mail.com, they have templates that you can customize and typically have good phone support to assist in getting these mailings created if you need help.

Another print item may be what I (and others) refer to as the "yellow letter." The yellow letter is literally an 8.5" x 11" sheet of yellow pad paper with lines on with a simple message to a home owner about wanting to buy their house. With a hand written address on the envelope and the hand written yellow letter inside, it looks very personal, and will get sellers to call you. There are even services that will print these envelopes and letters so that you don't have to hand write them.

When home sellers respond to your mailing and call or email you, be prepared with the questions you will need to ask them to collect information about the house they want to sell. Scripts that I use and what to say to sellers can be found at RVRealEstateIncome.com

Telephone or telemarketing campaigns can also be done from wherever you are, assuming you have good cell phone service.

Again, creating a list or finding potential home sellers to call is the first step with a telemarketing campaign. Finding owners that want to sell their home can be found on web sites such as Craigslist.com, Zillow.com, various For Sale By Owner sites, Expired listings from real estate agents to name a few.

You will want to have a script to follow when speaking with these sellers also. With the right script you will be able to determine how motivated they are, and if they are a good candidate for referring to a real estate agent or investor that you are working with. This is a good way to generate leads for yourself if you are wanting to purchase or wholesale houses.

Online campaigns would include having a web site letting visitors to the site know that you want to buy their house or in general want to help them get their house sold, if they are wanting to sell. To get an idea of a site like this, just search for "Sell my ……… house fast" and see what pops up.

Creating an online marketing campaign with Google Adwords, Facebook, or other traffic generating means will hopefully drive home owners that want to sell their house to your site.

Online marketing to generate leads from motivated home sellers is very competitive. You will want to spend some time researching what is already online and attempt to come up with ideas that are unique so that you can stand out from the crowd.

If you are not tech savvy and have no interest learning this, you can find people that are at sites like Upwork.com, or Fiverr.com. There are people on these sites that work from their own virtual office (maybe an RV) and provide services to others.

The leads that you generate may be able to sold to real estate agents or investors depending on the quality of leads and the potential buyers of the leads you can find.

Realize that in most areas you will not be able to be paid on only leads that turn into deals for the investor or listings for the agent because of state laws and or regulations (unless you have a real estate license), but you should be able to find a way to structure a compensation model that works for you and the lead buyer, and is legal.

If you initially don't find an agent or investor that is willing to work out a compensation model for generating leads, find a different agent or investor.

Having someone that is able to provide good quality leads of home owners that are motivated to sell their house is very valuable to both real estate agents and investors. You should be able to sell these leads for an average of $10 to $50 per lead, or more, depending on the market area and housing prices that you are generating leads in.

Good real estate agents and investors know that listing or buying houses is a numbers game. It takes talking to a certain number of sellers to generate a listing or house purchase. If you are providing them good leads, you can become a very valuable asset to them and in turn generate good compensation for yourself.

Another big benefit of this type of work is that you can be generating leads for any part of the country while camping anywhere in the country assuming you have good phone and internet connections.

If you combine this activity with what I consider the passive activity of having a real estate license discussed in Section 2, you can create a great way to realistically generate $2,000 to $5,000 or more per month. Would this help create the RV lifestyle of your dreams?

7

PROVIDE VIRTUAL SERVICES FOR REAL ESTATE AGENTS & INVESTORS

Providing services to real estate agents and investors virtually can encompass many different tasks.

Some tasks that I have virtual assistants perform or have had perform in the past are; Marketing list creation, telephone or telemarketing, or emailing, to find motivated sellers, launching marketing campaigns by mailing post cards and letters as well as Click2Mail.com, taking phone calls and collecting information from house sellers, entering house seller information into an online database and other forms of lead management, follow up phone calls to home sellers, and other tasks related to my company buying and selling houses.

There are also virtual assistants that perform tasks more specific to real estate agents such as file management to ensure listings and closings are handled smoothly so that the agents can do what they do best, marketing activities similar to those mentioned above, and any other tasks that someone can assist an agent with to make the agent's business run smoother and more efficiently.

If you are more creative or tech savvy, some virtual services that I utilize and that are offered include brochure or flyer creation, web site creation (specifically for real estate agents and investors), assistants with social content like Facebook or LinkedIn.

These services will typically be paid on an hourly basis and will vary depending on your abilities and value to the particular agent or investor. Some virtual services charge from $30 to $125 per hour depending on the services they offer and demand for those services.

To get more ideas on what virtual services you could possibly provide, just go to an online site like Upwork.com and search for "real estate virtual assistant" to see what pops up. It will give you numerous ideas that might fit your abilities and desired amount of time you want to devote to these tasks.

You can also list yourself as a freelancer on sites like Upwork.com so that people wanting a virtual assistant will see your availability and skills.

Providing virtual assistant services should also give you some flexibility with your schedule instead of having a fixed schedule at an office.

Providing great virtual assistant services is a very valuable commodity to real estate agents and investors. I know from my own business that it is very beneficial to have virtual assistants that do a great job and provide great service to myself and my clients.

One way to determine what services are in demand is to call several investors and real estate agents in a particular market area and ask them what type of services they would like someone else to do, so that they can focus on the tasks that make them the most money.

I would recommend that if you want to provide virtual assistant services that you create an actual company with a separate tax identification number from you personally. This shows a potential services purchaser that you are "in business" and take this seriously.

8

CREATE CONTENT FOR REAL ESTATE AGENTS & INVESTORS

If you have creative writing or copywriting talents and abilities, generating content and copy for direct mail (letters and post cards), advertising, web sites, landing pages, blogs, etc. could be a good way to generate income.

As mentioned in the last chapter, this type of work is also typically billed as hourly. I have purchased these types of services from virtual assistants at $45 or more per hour.

Having unique content is important for investors and agents to set themselves apart from their competition. In my business, I am always looking for ways to give a house seller a reason to call me instead of other investors or agents.

Marketing and advertising have become much more than just creating a simple ad to give a person an idea that someone is in business. To be effective, a person needs to provide good, educational content so that someone needing real estate services gets real value in the content we are providing and because of that content, seeks us out to do business with.

You can also advertise that you provide these types of services on web sites such as Upwork.com and Fiverr.com. As in the last chapter, you can see what kinds of services others are providing and services that are being requested.

SECTION 2

PASSIVE INCOME GENERATION

In this section we will discuss several ways to generate a truly passive income. Some do take an initial effort of finding or securing the investment but once made will generate a passive income that doesn't require much, if any, time or effort.

This is the type of income that I and hopefully you strive to create. This is the type of income that allows a person to live the RV lifestyle of their dreams.

9

BUYING RENTAL HOUSES

Buying single family houses as rental property is probably the most common form of real estate investing for passive income.

However, when considering this type of investment, most people immediately respond with "but I don't want to fix toilets or get calls from tenants in the middle of the night." I don't want to fix toilets or get calls from tenants in the middle of the night (or ever) either. There are ways to avoid these hands on management issues, which we will discuss shortly.

First, why single family houses? For anyone wanting to "invest" in real estate, I think a person gravitates to wanting multi family properties such as apartment houses (that used to be my goal). It may appear better to have 30 "doors" with one property instead of 30 individual houses, but after 20 years of real estate activity, I'd rather have the single family houses.

It may be easier to buy one apartment building rather than 30 individual houses, but I'd still rather have the houses.

Management of apartments are typically more labor intensive than good single family houses. Tenants of apartments tend to move more which creates more turnover costs than good tenants of houses that want to make a house their "home."

Investing in apartments may look good on paper, but in reality, I'd prefer single family houses.

The first issue to consider is the purchase, or acquisition of a property.

As discussed in Chapter 3 about Selecting A Market Area, determining location is very important, and definitely more important when keeping a house as a rental. If I buy and resell, it's important to have a good resalable neighborhood, but if I am buying a property for a rental, I want to know it will attract a good tenant and be a good investment house for a long time.

The location inside of a particular market area is also extremely important. You want to have a rental house in areas where people WANT to live, not HAVE to live because they have no other choices.

Areas that have good schools, churches, or other reasons to attract good tenants are important.

I would typically want a 3 or 4 bedroom house as a rental. I do have some 2 bedroom houses, but that limits who your renters will be. Also, I would not have more than 4, as this might invite a larger number of tenants staying in the house which may lead to increased wear and tear on the house.

Having a garage is very beneficial. Tenants tend to have a lot of "stuff" and want a place to store it.

You want rental houses that are not "goofy" or functionally obsolete. If you have to walk through one bedroom to get to the bathroom or another bedroom, I would pass.

I would stay away from owning rental houses that are on busy streets. Most people don't want to have a family on a busy street.

I would try to select houses that were built in 1978 or newer. Houses built prior to 1978 may contain lead paint. Although I do have rentals built before 1978, my preference would be to have newer houses. I am continually working to sell my older rentals so that I only have rental houses built in 1978 or newer.

The price range of houses I want as rentals is similar to prices mentioned in Chapter 3. In my markets I can typically buy a 3 bedroom house in a decent neighborhood for $60,000 to $150,000 (usually plus some cost for updating) that will rent for $700 to $1,500 per month.

Expenses of a rental house will typically equal 40% to 50% of the gross amount of rent. Rental house expenses are Property Taxes, Insurance, Vacancy, Maintenance, and Management. These expenses do not include any debt service, or loan payments.

I would expect to receive 40% to 50% of the gross rents as "net" income as a return on my investment, if I paid cash for the house. This income should equal a 6% to 12% or better return on my cash investment, if using all cash, to purchase the rental house.

For example, if I used $100,000 cash to purchase a house, I would expect at least a $500 per month NET return on that investment.

I would not want loan payments for the purchase of the rental house to be more than 25% to 35% of the gross rents. If your payments are more than this, the rental house can quickly become a property that costs you money each month instead of providing any type of passive income.

You may read other authors that calculate their investment return on a small down payment, and then borrow the majority of the purchase with a loan. I do not think that is a good way to calculate a return on your investment.

Using "good" debt in the acquisition of rental properties may be necessary or advantageous financially. However, when considering how good of an investment a particular property is, I still calculate my return as if I paid cash for the house.

These other authors will also usually assume some appreciation and tax savings as a return on your investment. Although important, I would rather those items just be icing on the cake and not count on appreciation or tax savings when deciding how good of an investment a rental house is.

10

OWNING PARTS OF RENTAL HOUSES

One way to get a little exposure to owning a rental house without the financial risk is to own part of a rental house.

Locate and get a potentially great rental property under contract, then find a buyer for that property that would want to keep the property as a rental. Then instead of just taking a "wholesaler" fee to sell the contract, negotiate with the buyer to receive a monthly amount as well as possibly an amount in the event the property is sold.

The details of this type of arrangement could be anything that you can imagine and negotiate with your buyer of the property. This will heavily depend on how good of a deal you find and can pass along to the investor/buyer.

In return for finding a great rental for an investor, you could create an agreement where the investor would pay you $50 to $100 per month depending on the house being rented or not, and 10% of the gross proceeds when the house is sold.

The above is just one example of what could be negotiated.

The best part about these arrangements are that once one is in place, it can continue to provide a monthly income with no additional work. Could 9 or 10 of these agreements improve your RV lifestyle?

11

PRIVATE LENDING

Private lending is basically "being the bank" for other investors. There are numerous situations where investors would rather work with private lenders than traditional banks and lenders, and pay what would be perceived as above market interest rates.

When investors buy and resell houses, the access to money to fund their deals is more important than the interest rate they will pay. When an investor finds a "deal" the cost of money is somewhat insignificant compared to the ability to have access to money to be able to buy and close on the deal.

Its not uncommon for private lenders being able to charge 8% to 12% interest (or sometimes more) in situations like this.

The downside of these loans for the private lender is that the investor doesn't need the funds for very long, typically 3 to 6 months. With these types of deals the investor wants to buy and resell as quickly as possible. This is also why paying 6% or 12% interest for a few months doesn't make much difference on the investor's net profit of the deal.

As a private lender, you want to have your money working for you all the time, not just a couple months here and a couple months there.

To protect yourself, you could have a 6 month minimum loan to the investor. That way, no matter how short of time the investor has your money, you will get paid 6 months' interest.

There are other lending arrangements where the lender may get a lower interest rate plus a percentage of profits. This type of arrangement would be more common in situations where the lender may be providing assistance or financial guidance to the investor. In most situations, the private lender just wants interest payments without the hassle of participating in a real estate deal.

Even in situations where an investor wants to buy and hold, paying 4% to 6% interest to a private lender in todays markets is sometimes more advantageous than having to go through a traditional lender.

In any of the above scenarios it may be beneficial to the investor and private lender to create loans with interest only payments. The benefit to the investor/borrower is lower monthly payments. The benefit to the private lender is that their principal is deployed and working and they don't have to worry about the math of amortizing a loan.

The two things you MUST know when being a private lender: Who you are lending money to, and the property that will be used as security for your loan.

Who you are lending money to as a private lender is almost as important as the property being used as collateral for the loan. Do you know the borrower? Have they been working with real estate for some time and have a good track record? If they don't have a lot of experience with real estate or just getting started, do you have other ways to check how trustworthy and credit worthy they are? How likely are they to keep their word and pay you back according to your agreement?

The property being used as security or collateral should be property that you wouldn't mind owning (or that someone else wouldn't mind owning) if the borrower defaults on the loan and you have to foreclose and take the property back by legal means. There is a saying in the private lender world that reflects this – loan to own.

Two other additional items you want to ensure when being a private lender; 1) always get title insurance to ensure your lien position on the property. And 2) always have the borrower purchase property insurance and name you or your lending entity as the beneficiary on the insurance policy.

Private lenders typically do not want to own the property they are lending money on, but you have to be prepared for the worst case scenario. Working with borrowers as discussed above will help eliminate the unwanted situations of having to take a property back from the borrower.

Where do you find borrowers for these types of loans? A few ways to locate potential borrowers would be from real estate agents, title and closing companies, and real estate investor groups.

Real estate agents that work with investors. There are agents that work with investors as a bigger percentage of their business than other agents. You could do a search for these types of agents. You could also call a broker's office and ask if they have agents that work exclusively or extensively with investors. These agents most likely know investors that may have a need for private lender funds.

Title and closing companies. These companies that close real estate transactions will often know of individuals that borrow or would like to have private lender resources to borrow money from. Title and closing companies should also have the connections to create the loan documents and properly secure your loans with a particular property and provide title insurance for your loan, that the borrower pays for.

Both real estate agents and the title/closing companies would be able to provide information on investor/borrowers about how long they've been in business, how much business an investor is doing, etc.

Most cities and metro areas have real estate investor groups or associations. This may be a good place to meet investors, potential borrowers, and other individuals that have an interest in real estate. They may have other educational resources that you might find helpful.

Using retirement funds for private lending.

If you currently have retirement funds in a traditional retirement account, you can transfer these funds (or some of the funds) to a self directed IRA custodian and use them for private lending. There are a number of self directed IRA custodians, with **Quest IRA** being one example that I use.

The benefit to you is that you can use your retirement funds to invest in something you can control, and have much less risk when done properly than with other investment alternatives.

12

BUYING TAX LIENS

I'm assuming everyone reading this book is familiar with property taxes. When a property owner doesn't pay their property taxes, the local taxing authority creates a tax "lien" against the property.

Once a year, the local authorities will hold some version of an auction to sell these tax liens to investors.

The tax lien sales will generate income for the local government who would have otherwise not received the income to run the local government functions.

Every state is different, but the interest rate the property owner has to pay is typically well above interest rates being offered at a local bank. I have purchased tax liens that paid 14% to 24% interest, based on an annual interest rate. The property owner has to pay this interest if they want to clear the tax lien from their property.

A buyer of a tax lien will typically have to wait a certain amount of time (typically a few years) before they can start a legal action to either force the property owner to pay the taxes or have the property auctioned off. When the property is auctioned, you have the right to be a buyer or if someone bids more than you want to for the property, the tax lien with interest will be paid back first, before any other liens in most cases. Again, this process may vary from state to state.

The positives of tax liens:

The obvious item is the above market interest rate paid on tax liens.

A secondary item is the safety and security of the investment.

A third aspect which could be a negative, is that someone can invest just a few hundred or few thousand dollars, and when you can generate a 14% or more return, its just like investing much more capital at a lower interest rate.

The negatives of tax liens:

It's a challenge to invest more than what most investors would consider an adequate amount of capital for the time and effort involved. As mentioned below, it does take some time and effort researching properties with tax liens, which may not be worth it to someone that can only invest a few hundred or few thousand dollars.

I would highly recommend doing some homework about a property before buying a tax lien on the property. There are times where the reason that a person or entity hasn't paid taxes on a property is because it's worthless. You don't want to be stuck with a property or tax lien on a property that isn't worth the taxes owed against it.

The tax lien may be paid off quickly after the purchase or auction. A property owner can pay off the lien whenever they want and may choose to do so instead of incurring a high interest rate on their lien. As an investor, it may not be worth the time and effort to research the property, attend the sale to buy the tax lien, just to have the lien paid off within a few months after the sale.

If you have a self directed IRA or other retirement plan as mentioned in a previous chapter, you can use these funds to buy tax liens, making the investment tax free or deferred.

Before investing in tax liens check out the state and local county laws where you are considering investing to educate yourself thoroughly about this investment.

13

GET A REAL ESTATE LICENSE TO GENERATE REFERRAL INCOME

Just like the perceptions that come along with owning rental houses and being a landlord, most people (including myself) have or had misconceptions of what was included when having a real estate license.

For the first several years when I was in the business of buying and selling houses I didn't want to get a real estate license because of the thought of having to work with home buyers and sellers, showing houses, holding open houses, and especially working nights and week ends. I finally realized that I didn't have to do any of those tasks.

Each state has their unique requirements of the amount of education is needed to be able to then take a test to become a licensed real estate agent. Checking with the real estate board of the state you officially reside in should be able to provide you the requirements needed. You may be able to become a licensed agent in a state that you do not reside in, but as with other items associated with real estate, you will need to check with that state's real estate commission to determine what is needed and the costs involved.

Also know that just because you have a real estate license does not necessarily mean that you need to join the board of Realtors or pay for access to the MLS to receive referral commissions. Check with your state's real estate commission for details.

Once you are a licensed agent in one state, you can generate referral commissions from any state. This gives you the ability to generate leads and referrals from one state while camping in different states.

There are a few reasons why I secured and still have a license today.

One of the initial reasons for getting a real estate license more than 15 years ago, was to have access to the Multiple Listing Service (MLS). Although there are now multiple online options to research values of houses, at that time and even now, I consider the MLS the best source for determining house values. Even with the other options for determining values, most buyers who are represented by an agent, will use the MLS to determine values of a house they are considering buying.

A second reason was to be able to access Expired listings in the MLS. Although a person can usually find an agent that will supply this information, I would rather have the ability to research this information to create my own list for marketing purposes. Expired Listings are sometimes a good list to market to.

Probably the biggest reason to have a real estate license, that I didn't realize for years, is the ability to refer buyers and sellers to other agents that I have a relationship or affiliation with to generate referral commissions for myself.

For years I would do the work and spend the money necessary to generate leads of home sellers that would call me wanting to sell their house. But if I couldn't buy their house, I would just throw the lead in the trash. Looking back, I have no idea how much money I essentially threw away.

Now when I generate leads, if I can't buy the house, I will offer the home seller the services of my affiliated agents to market (list) their house. When the seller lists their house with the agent and the house sells, I receive a referral commission.

The amount of the referral commission is typically at least 25% of the total commission that my affiliated agent would receive for listing the property. This is usually 1% (or close to 1%) of the sale price of the house. The sale of a $100,000 house would generate an approximately $1,000 referral commission for you.

The same arrangement can apply for referring leads to agents for home buyers.

There is more information in regards to getting a real estate license at RVRealEstateIncome.com

This can be a passive activity, but if combined with the active item of generating leads in the first section, can be a great way to realistically generate $2,000 to $5,000 or more per month. Would this help create the RV lifestyle of your dreams?

SECTION 3

BONUS RESOURCES

14

FINANCING OPTIONS WHEN BUYING HOUSES

There are a few options available when it comes to financing the purchase of houses. From your own savings, borrowing from a bank or traditional lender, borrowing from a private lender (as mentioned in a previous chapter), or having the seller finance the purchase for you.

From your own savings.

If you have the financial resources, using these funds for the purchase of real estate may be a much better way to generate income from these funds than with other investments.

If you can buy a rental house with your savings and generate a 6% to 12% (or more) return on your money, is this better than what you can accomplish with other investments?

Other benefits of this investment is that you can control it. You are not just giving your money to some person or entity you have never met and trusting them to take care of and grow your investment savings.

With a rental house, you have a "real" asset. Its not a piece of paper that is worth something one day and then worth much less or nothing the next.

If you have savings that enable you to act quickly to buy a house, you have an advantage over other buyers that have to get a loan and make offers based on that contingency.

Borrowing from a bank or traditional lender.

Borrowing funds from a bank or traditional lender is the typical way that most people think of when wanting funds to buy a property. Like any option, this has positive and negative aspects.

One positive is that banks have money to lend. This is their business.

Traditional lenders like this are about the only option for getting long term, fixed rate loans. Even as an investor, you can usually access 20 or 30 year, fixed rate loans for single family houses.

One negative is that it does typically take jumping through a number of hoops to be qualified before securing a loan. You have to fill out a bunch of paperwork, your credit is checked, the property has to be appraised, etc. This process can take weeks to complete. If you had your sites on a great deal, someone with access to cash may have already bought the property before you can secure the loan.

You will be somewhat limited to how many rental properties you can buy depending on the type of traditional financing you have on these properties.

It may take time, but building a relationship with a bank is the best way I know to overcome some of the negatives of working with a traditional lender.

I also think its beneficial to work with a small, local bank instead of one of the large national banks. This way they get to really know you instead of just being a faceless number to them.

Private lenders.

Private lenders may be friends, family members, or others that have savings and would like to lend these funds to you to buy real estate.

When I started my career of buying and selling houses, I approached a couple of my friends/neighbors about borrowing money from them. Because they knew me, and knew their investment would be secured with a lien on the property, they took a chance to lend money to me. I still borrow funds from a couple of these individuals today.

One reason an individual would lend money in this manner is because it allows them to earn an above average return on their investment and also be very secure, since it is backed by a real piece of property.

Being a private lender gives an investor the opportunity to participate in the real estate market without having to do anything "hands on."

From a borrowers perspective, one positive is that I have never had to jump through "hoops" with the private lenders I've worked with. Either they decided to invest funds with me or not. There was no filling out a bunch of paperwork to see if they thought I was a good risk.

You can discuss and create loan terms that make sense for both of you instead of just going with the terms dictated to you by a traditional lender.

You typically should not have to pay any "points" or other loan initiation fees or expenses when working with a private lender, unless the lender is also going to receive some percentage of the profits from a transaction.

Seller financing.

Having the seller finance the sale of their house to you is the best way I know of to purchase a house.

It is customary and typically expected that when a person sells their house, they want cash from the sale. But there are exceptions.

Why would a seller finance the purchase of their house when they sell?

I've worked with numerous sellers that wanted to sell their house but didn't NEED the proceeds of the sale in the form of cash. When I offer to buy a house from a seller, I usually offer them one price with a cash offer, and another higher price if they are willing to take payments for the house. I let them know that I can pay an overall higher price for the house if it's easier for me (by making payment) to buy the house (than with having to come up with cash). The seller sometimes decides that they would rather receive the higher price with payments offer instead of the lower cash offer.

Sometimes a seller's house is such poor condition that a buyer would not be able to secure a loan to purchase the house. Either the seller has to do repairs and updates to the house or they need to finance the purchase of the house for a buyer, if they want to sell.

When sellers are willing to sell their house with seller financing, I would typically want to keep these houses for rentals unless there are other reasons why the particular house would not be a good rental.

Also know that if you locate a house and the seller is willing to finance the sale, this "deal" can be sold and transferred to another buyer, just like a wholesale deal discussed earlier in the book. I would be willing to pay some amount of money to purchase a contract where the seller was willing to finance the sale of their house. Check RVRealEstateIncome.com for more information.

When creating a transaction like this, make sure the monthly payments are no more than 30% to 40% of what the monthly gross rental amount would be. You want to ensure that this would be a rental with a positive cash flow for yourself or a buyer of the contract.

15

LOCATING PROPERTIES TO BUY AND RESELL OR HOLD AS RENTALS

Because the subject of locating properties pertains both to the Buy and Resell as well as the Buy and Hold for Rental chapters, I will address the topic in its own chapter.

This topic will actually apply to almost all the other active and some passive ways to generate income addressed in this book.

One of the most important things to understand is that great deals do not just come to you, you have to create them. If you wait for someone, especially a real estate agent, to bring you a great deal, you may be waiting a long time to achieve the RV lifestyle of your dreams.

In the approximately 20 years that I have been buying and selling houses, real estate agents have brought me less than 10 "deals," and most of these were in the couple of years after the market crash of 2008.

Since I generated leads that led to the houses that I purchased from my "remote" home location in Lincoln, NE and before that my family farm in south central Nebraska, know that you can generate leads from your RV wherever you happen to be.

You can use the information provided in Chapters 3 and 6 to determine who you target and how you get your message in front of them.

As in Chapter 3, you need to determine geographically where you want to locate and possibly buy houses, or locate houses for others that want to buy. If you're trying to locate deals for others, you will obviously want to know where they want to buy houses and then focus on those areas.

As discussed in Chapter 6, once you know where your potential house sellers are, you want to get your message that you (or those you are generating leads for) are interested in buying houses in their neighborhood. The message should include benefits of why they should call you if they want to sell.

You can also find home sellers at the multiple for sale by owner web sites and call or email them.

In any type of marketing discussion, the 3 legs of a "marketing stool" are market, media, and message. Know who you want to target, determine how you are going to target them (TV, radio, post cards, yellow letters, online, calling For Sale By Owner ads, etc.), and determine the best message to get your "target" to respond to your offer.

Know that with any type of marketing campaign to find house sellers, you will need to get your message in front of your target most likely multiple times before they will respond. You may get lucky, but don't expect calls from sellers from just one mailing or contact.

The more precise the list, and the more tailored a message is to that list, the better chance that you will have sellers respond and contact you.

This may seem like a lot of work, and sometimes it is, but as I said earlier, if you want to be successful at finding "deals" you have to generate those leads and create the "deal." Great deals seldom just come along on their own.

Most importantly, know that by being able to successfully and consistently generate house seller (and buyer) leads, you really can live the RV lifestyle of your dreams.

16

TAX BENEFITS

First, let me state that I am not a CPA or anyone that you should take tax information and guidance from.

I will tell you that depending on your business activities mentioned in this book, that you perform from your RV, you should discuss if and how this can benefit you from a tax standpoint with your CPA or other qualified person.

Some of the activities discussed would typically create "earned" income whereas other activities would create "passive" income or capital gains. Knowing how each of these will directly effect your situation is important and something I would highly encourage you to know.

17

SUMMARY

I want to thank you for reading this book. I am confident that if you really want to create an RV lifestyle of your dreams, this book and I can help.

Even if you know nothing about real estate right now, hopefully this book has given you some ideas on what is possible for you to generate income from your RV.

All of the different tasks and investing methods mentioned in this book are things that I do or have others assist my business with. These are real activities that you can do also.

My goal with this book was to provide you an overview of what is possible, although it may seem a little overwhelming right now. For those that would like to learn more and take the next step to live the RV lifestyle of your dreams, check out www.RVRealEstateIncome.com.

As a special Thank You for reading this book, I would like to make you a special offer to join RVRealEstateIncome.com.

For a limited time, use the code "Real Estate" at the web site to receive a very special offer when you join.

Thank you again, and I wish you the best with your RV Lifestyle.

ABOUT THE AUTHOR

Ben Souchek is the foremost authority for anyone wanting to learn how to generate income, working with real estate, virtually and remotely to create the RV lifestyle of their dreams.

Ben purchased his first rental property at the age of 21. Started his company, The Sierra Group, LLC, to buy and sell houses at the age of 30 in 1997, and continues to buy and sell houses even from the comfort of his family's RV today.

He has purchased hundreds of houses and generated hundreds of leads that he has referred to real estate agents that he has worked with.

He has also been a licensed real estate agent for more than 15 years.

Ben was driven to create this book due to his own interest of wanting his family to enjoy the lifestyle of travelling in an RV, and still generate the income needed to travel and live well, and to show others how they can enjoy the RV lifestyle of their dreams.

DISCLOSURES AND DISCLAIMERS

All trademarks and service marks are the intellectual properties of their respective owners. All references to these properties are made solely for editorial purposes. Except for marks actually owned by Ben Souchek ("Souchek") or The Sierra Group LLC, a Nebraska limited liability company ("Sierra Group"), no commercial claims are made to their use, and neither Souchek nor Sierra Group is affiliated with such marks in any way.

Unless otherwise expressly noted, none of the individuals or business entities mentioned herein has endorsed the contents of this real estate book.

Limits of Liability & Disclaimers of Warranties
Because this real estate book is a general educational information product, it is not a substitute for professional advice on the topics discussed in it.

The materials in this real estate book are provided "as is" and without warranties of any kind either express or implied. Souchek and Sierra Group disclaim all warranties, express or implied, including, but not limited to, implied warranties of merchantability and fitness for a particular purpose. Souchek and Sierra Group do not warrant that defects will be corrected. Souchek does not warrant or make any representations regarding the use or the results of the use of the materials in this book in terms of their correctness, accuracy, reliability, or otherwise. Applicable law may not allow the exclusion of implied warranties, so the above exclusion may not apply to you.

Under no circumstances, including, but not limited to, negligence, shall Souchek or Sierra Group be liable for any special or consequential damages that result from the use of, or the inability to use this book, even if Souchek, Sierra Group, or an authorized representative has been advised of the possibility of such damages. Applicable law may not allow the limitation or exclusion of liability or incidental or consequential damages, so the above limitation or exclusion may not apply to you. In no event shall Souchek or Sierra Group total liability to you for all damages, losses, and causes of action (whether in contract, tort, including but not limited to, negligence or otherwise) exceed the amount paid by you, if any, for this book.

You agree to hold Souchek and Sierra Group of this book, principals, agents, affiliates, employees, successors, and assigns harmless from any and all liability for all claims for damages due to injuries, including attorney fees and costs, incurred by you or caused to third parties by you, arising out of the products, services, and activities discussed in this real estate book, excepting only claims for gross negligence or intentional tort.

You agree that any and all claims for gross negligence or intentional tort shall be settled solely by confidential binding arbitration per the American Arbitration Association's commercial arbitration rules. The law of the State of Nebraska shall govern. Your claim cannot be aggregated with third party claims. All arbitration must occur in the City of Lincoln, State of Nebraska. Arbitration fees and costs shall be split equally, and you are solely responsible for your own lawyer fees.

Facts and information are believed to be accurate at the time they were placed in this book. All data provided in this book is to be used for information purposes only. The information contained within is not intended to provide specific legal, financial, tax, physical or mental health advice, or any other advice whatsoever, for any individual or company and should not be relied upon in that regard. The services described are only offered in jurisdictions where they may be legally offered. Information provided is not all-inclusive, and is limited to information that is made available and such information should not be relied upon as all-inclusive or accurate.

For more information about this policy, please contact Souchek via the contact information found in the Copyright Notice at the front of this book.

IF YOU DO NOT AGREE WITH THESE TERMS AND EXPRESS CONDITIONS, DO NOT READ THIS BOOK. YOUR USE OF THIS BOOK, INCLUDING PRODUCTS, SERVICES, AND ANY PARTICIPATION IN ACTIVITIES MENTIONED IN THIS BOOK, MEAN THAT YOU ARE AGREEING TO BE LEGALLY BOUND BY THESE TERMS.

Affiliate Compensation & Material Connections Disclosure
This book may contain references to websites and information created and maintained by other individuals and organizations. Souchek and Sierra Group do not control or guarantee the accuracy, completeness, relevance, or timeliness of any information or privacy policies posted on these websites.

You should assume that all references to products and services in this book are made because material connections exist between Souchek or Sierra Group and the providers of the mentioned products and services ("Provider"). You should also assume that all website links within this book are affiliate links for (a) Souchek, (b) Sierra

Group, or (c) someone else who is an affiliate for the mentioned products and services (individually and collectively, the "Affiliate").

The Affiliate recommends products and services in this book based in part on a good faith belief that the purchase of such products or services will help readers in general.

The Affiliate has this good faith belief because (a) the Affiliate has tried the product or service mentioned prior to recommending it or (b) the Affiliate has researched the reputation of the Provider and has made the decision to recommend the Provider's products or services based on the Provider's history of providing these or other products or services.

The representations made by the Affiliate about products and services reflect the Affiliate's honest opinion based upon the facts known to the Affiliate at the time this book was published.

Because there is a material connection between the Affiliate and Providers of products or services mentioned in this book, you should always assume that the Affiliate may be biased because of the Affiliate's relationship with a Provider and/or because the Affiliate has received or will receive something of value from a Provider.

Perform your own due diligence before purchasing real estate, a product, or a service mentioned in this book.

The type of compensation received by the Affiliate may vary. In some instances, the Affiliate may receive complimentary products (such as a review copy), services, or money from a Provider prior to mentioning the Provider's products or services in this book.

In addition, the Affiliate may receive a monetary commission or non-monetary compensation when you take action by using a website link within in this book. This includes, but is not limited to, when you purchase a product or service from a Provider after going to a website link contained in this book.

Earnings & Income Disclaimers

No Earnings Projections, Promises or Representations
For purposes of these disclaimers, the term "Souchek" refers individually and collectively to the author of this book and to the affiliate (if any) whose affiliate hyperlinks are referenced in this book.

You recognize and agree that Souchek and Sierra Group have made no implications, warranties, promises, suggestions, projections, representations or guarantees whatsoever to you about future prospects or earnings, or that you will earn any money, with respect to your purchase of this book, and that Souchek and Sierra Group have not authorized any such projection, promise, or representation by others.

Any earnings or income statements, or any earnings or income examples, are only estimates of what you *might* earn. There is no assurance you will do as well as stated in any examples. If you rely upon any figures provided, you must accept the entire risk of not doing as well as the information provided. This applies whether the earnings or income examples are monetary in nature or pertain to advertising credits which may be earned (whether such credits are convertible to cash or not).

There is no assurance that any prior successes or past results as to earnings or income (whether monetary or advertising credits, whether convertible to cash or not) will apply, nor can any prior successes be used, as an indication of your future success or results from any of the information, content, or strategies. Any and all claims or representations as to income or earnings (whether monetary or advertising credits, whether convertible to cash or not) are not to be considered as "average earnings".

Testimonials & Examples
Testimonials and examples in this book are exceptional results, do not reflect the typical purchaser's experience, do not apply to the average person and are not intended to represent or guarantee that anyone will achieve the same or similar results. Where specific income or earnings (whether monetary or advertising credits, whether convertible to cash or not), figures are used and attributed to a specific individual or business, that individual or business has earned that amount. There is no assurance that you will do as well using the same information or strategies. If you rely on the specific income or earnings figures used, you must accept all the risk of not doing as well. The described experiences are atypical. Your financial results are likely to differ from those described in the testimonials.

The Economy
The economy, where you do business, on a national and even worldwide scale, creates additional uncertainty and economic risk in real estate markets. An economic recession or depression might negatively affect your results.

Your Success or Lack of It
Your success in using the information or strategies provided in this real estate book depends on a variety of factors. Souchek and Sierra Group have no way of knowing how well you will do because they do not know you, your real estate experience, your background, your work ethic, your dedication, your motivation, your desire, or your business skills or practices. Therefore, neither Souchek nor Sierra Group guarantees or implies that you will get rich, that you will do as well, or that you will have any earnings (whether monetary or advertising credits, whether convertible to cash or not), at all.

Businesses and earnings derived therefrom, including real estate investments, involve unknown risks and are not suitable for everyone. You may not rely on any information presented in this book or otherwise provided by Souchek or Sierra Group, unless you do so with the knowledge and understanding that you can experience significant losses (including, but not limited to, the loss of any monies paid to purchase this book and/or any monies spent setting up, operating, and/or marketing your business activities, and further, that you may have no earnings at all (whether monetary or advertising credits, whether convertible to cash or not).

Forward-Looking Statements
Materials in this book may contain information that includes or is based upon forward-looking statements within the meaning of the Securities Litigation Reform Act of 1995. Forward-looking statements give Souchek's expectations or forecasts of future events. You can identify these statements by the fact that they do not relate strictly to historical or current facts. They use words such as "anticipate," "estimate," "expect," "project," "intend," "plan," "believe," and other words and terms of similar meaning in connection with a description of potential earnings or financial performance.

Any and all forward looking statements here or on any materials in this book are intended to express an opinion of earnings potential. Many factors will be important in determining your actual results and no guarantees are made that you will achieve results similar to Souchek or anybody else. In fact, no guarantees are made that you will achieve any results from applying Souchek's ideas, strategies, and tactics found in this book.

Purchase Price
Although Sierra Group believes the price is fair for the value that you receive, you understand and agree that the purchase price for this

book has been arbitrarily set by Sierra Group or the vendor who sold you this book. This price bears no relationship to objective standards.

Due Diligence
You are advised to do your own due diligence when it comes to making any decisions. Use caution and seek the advice of qualified professionals before acting upon the contents of this book or any other information. You shall not consider any examples, documents, or other content in this book or otherwise provided by Souchek or Sierra Group to be the equivalent of professional advice.

Souchek and Sierra Group assume no responsibility for any losses or damages resulting from your use of any link, information, or opportunity contained in this book or within any other information disclosed by Souchek or Sierra Group in any form whatsoever.

YOU SHOULD ALWAYS CONDUCT YOUR OWN INVESTIGATION (PERFORM DUE DILIGENCE) BEFORE BUYING PRODUCTS OR SERVICES FROM ANYONE. THIS INCLUDES PRODUCTS AND SERVICES SOLD VIA WEBSITE LINKS REFERENCED IN THIS REAL ESTATE BOOK.

NOTES

www.ingramcontent.com/pod-product-compliance
Lightning Source LLC
Chambersburg PA
CBHW070111210526
45170CB00013B/814